NORTH AMERICAN ANIMALS

# Roadrunners

by Christina Leighton

BLASTOFF! READERS

3

BELLWETHER MEDIA • MINNEAPOLIS, MN

Note to Librarians, Teachers, and Parents:

**Blastoff! Readers** are carefully developed by literacy experts and combine standards-based content with developmentally appropriate text.

**Level 1** provides the most support through repetition of high-frequency words, light text, predictable sentence patterns, and strong visual support.

**Level 2** offers early readers a bit more challenge through varied simple sentences, increased text load, and less repetition of high-frequency words.

**Level 3** advances early-fluent readers toward fluency through increased text and concept load, less reliance on visuals, longer sentences, and more literary language.

**Level 4** builds reading stamina by providing more text per page, increased use of punctuation, greater variation in sentence patterns, and increasingly challenging vocabulary.

**Level 5** encourages children to move from "learning to read" to "reading to learn" by providing even more text, varied writing styles, and less familiar topics.

Whichever book is right for your reader, Blastoff! Readers are the perfect books to build confidence and encourage a love of reading that will last a lifetime!

This edition first published in 2017 by Bellwether Media, Inc.

No part of this publication may be reproduced in whole or in part without written permission of the publisher. For information regarding permission, write to Bellwether Media, Inc., Attention: Permissions Department, 5357 Penn Avenue South, Minneapolis, MN 55419.

Library of Congress Cataloging-in-Publication Data

Names: Leighton, Christina, author.
Title: Roadrunners / by Christina Leighton.
Other titles: Blastoff! Readers. 3, North American Animals.
Description: Minneapolis, MN : Bellwether Media, Inc., 2017. | Series:
   Blastoff! Readers. North American Animals | Audience: Ages 5-8. |
   Audience: K to grade 3. | Includes bibliographical references and index.
Identifiers: LCCN 2016032046 (print) | LCCN 2016043055 (ebook) | ISBN
   9781626175686 (hardcover : alk. paper) | ISBN 9781681032894 (ebook)
Subjects: LCSH: Roadrunner-Juvenile literature.
Classification: LCC QL696.C83 L45 2017 (print) | LCC QL696.C83 (ebook) | DDC
   598.7/4-dc23
LC record available at https://lccn.loc.gov/2016032046

Editor: Betsy Rathburn     Designer: Brittany McIntosh

# Table of Contents

| | |
|---|---|
| What Are Roadrunners? | 4 |
| Agile Attackers | 12 |
| Chasing Mates | 16 |
| Racing Chicks | 18 |
| Glossary | 22 |
| To Learn More | 23 |
| Index | 24 |

# What Are Roadrunners?

Roadrunners are famous **cuckoo** birds in North America. They are often seen in dry **climates**.

## In the Wild

N
W    E
S

Extinct

Extinct in the Wild

Critically Endangered

Endangered

Vulnerable

Near Threatened

Least Concern

roadrunner range = ▢

conservation status: least concern

Deserts are home to many roadrunners. These birds also live in grasslands and other open areas.

## Identify a Roadrunner

**long tail**     **long legs**     **X-shaped feet**

Roadrunners often have brown and white feathers. Their **crests** sometimes stick up on top of their heads.

Their long legs help them run. Roadrunners use their long, straight tails to turn and stop.

crest

Roadrunners have feet with two toes in front and two in back. As they speed across the land, they leave X-shaped footprints behind.

Roadrunners can sprint more than 15 miles (24 kilometers) per hour. They prefer running or walking to flying.

There are two types of roadrunners.
Greater roadrunners are more
common than lesser roadrunners.
They are also larger in size.

greater
roadrunner

lesser
roadrunner

# Size of a Roadrunner

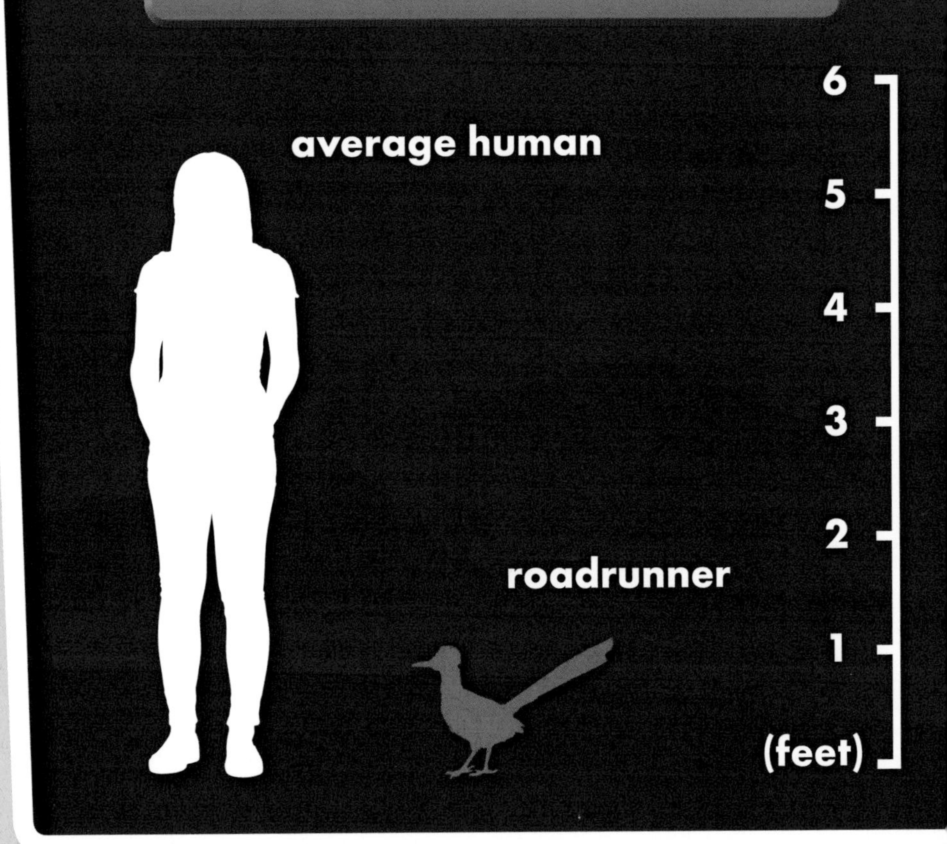

average human

roadrunner

6

5

4

3

2

1

(feet)

Roadrunners grow up to
12 inches (30 centimeters) tall.
Many weigh less than
1 pound (0.5 kilograms).

Roadrunners like to feed on fruits and small animals. These **omnivores** hit **prey** against the ground before they eat.

house sparrows

horned lizards

pocket mice

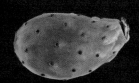

prickly pear cacti

western diamondback
rattlesnakes

American
grasshoppers

Lizards, mice, and birds are popular prey. Sometimes, roadrunners even catch snakes and scorpions!

red-tailed hawks

house cats

bobcats

coyotes

skunks

raccoons

Roadrunners watch out for coyotes and other **predators**.

These **agile** birds speed to safety.
Sharp turns also help them get away.

# Chasing Mates

Roadrunners perform **courtship displays**. Males and females share food and twigs.

Pairs often dance in a game of chase. Then the males **coo** and bow.

# Racing Chicks

A pair makes a nest together. The male gathers materials while the female builds. Soon, the female has a place to lay eggs.

## Baby Facts

| | |
|---|---|
| Name for babies: | chicks |
| Number of eggs laid: | 2 to 6 eggs |
| Time spent inside egg: | 18 to 20 days |
| Time spent with parents: | 30 to 40 days |

Both parents keep the eggs warm. After about three weeks, the **chicks** hatch.

The parents take turns feeding their chicks. In a month or two, the chicks are ready to race!

# Glossary

**agile**—able to quickly and easily move

**chicks**—baby roadrunners

**climates**—the specific weather conditions for certain areas

**coo**—to make a soft sound

**courtship displays**—behaviors that animals perform when choosing mates

**crests**—bunches of hair on top of roadrunners' heads

**cuckoo**—a group of birds known for their long tails

**omnivores**—animals that eat both plants and animals

**predators**—animals that hunt other animals for food

**prey**—animals that are hunted by other animals for food

# To Learn More

## AT THE LIBRARY

Alderfer, Jonathan K. *National Geographic Kids Bird Guide of North America: The Best Birding Book for Kids from National Geographic's Bird Experts.* Washington, D.C.: National Geographic, 2013.

Ganeri, Anita. *Roadrunner.* Chicago, Ill.: Heinemann Library, 2011.

Macken, JoAnn Early. *Roadrunners.* Pleasantville, N.Y.: Weekly Reader, 2010.

## ON THE WEB

Learning more about roadrunners is as easy as 1, 2, 3.

1. Go to www.factsurfer.com.

2. Enter "roadrunners" into the search box.

3. Click the "Surf" button and you will see a list of related web sites.

With factsurfer.com, finding more information is just a click away.

# Index

chicks, 19, 21

climates, 4

courtship displays, 16, 17

crests, 6, 7

cuckoo birds, 4

deserts, 5

eggs, 18, 19, 20

feathers, 6

feed, 12, 13, 21

feet, 6, 8

females, 16, 18

food, 12, 13, 16

footprints, 8

grasslands, 5

heads, 6

legs, 6, 7

males, 16, 17, 18

nest, 18

omnivores, 12

predators, 14

prey, 12, 13

range, 5

run, 7, 9

size, 10, 11

speed, 8, 9, 15

tails, 6, 7

toes, 8

types, 10

The images in this book are reproduced through the courtesy of: Steve Bower, front cover, p. 10 (top); John Cancalosi/ ard/ Age Fotostock, p. 4; Angel DiBilio, p. 6 (top left); Paul S. Wolf, p. 6 (top center); Hooplion, p. 6 (top right); Jill Fromer, p. 6 (bottom); Norman Bateman, p. 7; Danita Delimont/ Alamy Stock Photo, p. 8; blickwinkel/ Alamy Stock Photo, p. 9; FLPA/ Alamy Stock Photo, p. 10 (bottom); Alan Murphy/ BIA/ Minden Pictures/ SuperStock, p. 12; Eric Isselee, pp. 13 (top left), 14 (bottom left), 14 (bottom right); reptiles4all, p. 13 (top right); Charles A. Drost and Jan Hart/ Wikipedia, p. 13 (center left); Scisetti Alfio, p. 13 (center right); Audrey Snider-Bell, p. 13 (bottom left); http://www.birdphotos.com/ Wikipedia, p. 13 (bottom right); Le Do, p. 14 (top left); Chirtsova Natalia, p. 14 (top right); Svetlana Foote, p. 14 (center left); Cynthia Kidwell (center right); FLPA/ Neil Bowman/ Age Fotostock, p. 15; the4js, p. 16; gracious_tiger, p. 17; Charles Melton/ Alamy Stock Photo, p. 18; ZUMA Press Inc/ Alamy Stock Photo, p. 19; Rolf Nussbaumer/ Nature Picture Library, p. 20; Russ Nussbaumer/ Age Fotostock, p. 21.

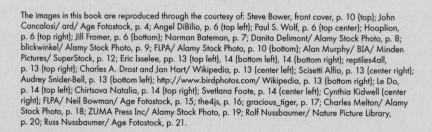